T0209731

WHAT HEALING MEANS TO ME

A Primer

Alexander T. Augoustides,
MD, ABIHM, FAAFP

BALBOA.
PRESS

A DIVISION OF HAY HOUSE

This book is a work of non-fiction. Unless otherwise noted, the author and the publisher make no explicit guarantees as to the accuracy of the information contained in this book and in some cases, names of people and places have been altered to protect their privacy.

Balboa Press books may be ordered through booksellers or by contacting:

Balboa Press
A Division of Hay House
1663 Liberty Drive
Bloomington, IN 47403
www.balboapress.com
1 (877) 407-4847

Because of the dynamic nature of the Internet, any web addresses or links contained in this book may have changed since publication and may no longer be valid. The views expressed in this work are solely those of the author and do not necessarily reflect the views of the publisher, and the publisher hereby disclaims any responsibility for them.

The author of this book does not dispense medical advice or prescribe the use of any technique as a form of treatment for physical, emotional, or medical problems without the advice of a physician, either directly or indirectly. The intent of the author is only to offer information of a general nature to help you in your quest for emotional and spiritual well-being. In the event you use any of the information in this book for yourself, which is your constitutional right, the author and the publisher assume no responsibility for your actions.

Any people depicted in stock imagery provided by Getty Images are models, and such images are being used for illustrative purposes only. Certain stock imagery © Getty Images.

Print information available on the last page.

ISBN: 978-1-9822-3187-3 (sc)
ISBN: 978-1-9822-3188-0 (e)

Balboa Press rev. date: 08/26/2019

CONTENTS

FOREWORD

My friend and colleague, "Dr. A," has created an introduction and a roadmap for you, a person seeking greater health. In doing so, Alex brings his unique personality, gifts, and insights to his task to successfully deliver to you this thoughtful work as a motivational and educational guide.

Dr. Augoustides' unique personality derives partly from his eclectic origins within the loving, nurturing and demonstrative Greek diaspora, resulting in Alex's ebullient way of connecting, lifting up, and I dare say actually loving the many humans in his life, in various forms of relationship whether family, friend, peer or client. I imagine that his personal history of being raised in a turbulent and tumultuous South Africa helped hone some of Dr. A's keen senses of pragmatism and real-world acumen, sharpening his impressive powers of observation and discernment. It is indeed one useful skill to be effusive in one's connection with a client, but Alex also leverages that high emotional IQ into motivational guidance and successful clinical outcomes for his clients through the application and leverage of his scientific intellect and his solid clinical protocols in Integrative Medicine.

This book, *What Healing Means to Me*, shares some of Alex's insights and learnings into the Why's, the What's and the How's of improving your health, with particular focus upon building and developing your skills in self-inquiry, self-observation and self-motivation in support of this goal. For too long, the conventional medical model has been for the physician to fix or manage the health challenges of the patient, therefore training most patients into a passive role. One aspect of Integrative Medicine is to awaken and support our clients' senses of autonomy and agency, inviting and even cajoling them into reclaiming their own personal power as the 'captain of the ship' along the cruise of their individual healing journey. Awakening back into self-empowerment is essential for any true healing, and Dr. A's real contribution here is delivering to you a wealth of insightful steps and tools towards your own self-empowerment.

I trust *What Healing Means to Me* will assist you in your own re-awakening into greater health.

James Biddle, MD

INTRODUCTION

Welcome and Thank You!

> *Life is a great big canvas, and you should throw all the paint on it you can.*
>
> *—Danny Kaye*

Welcome and thank you! This small book is an outline of a method and program that **works**.

In my experience, I have found that the majority of my patients need a plan that:

- Is uniquely tailored to their specific problem(s).
- Has a framework that is understandable.
- Is most importantly, **doable**.

So what I have tried to do over the last 20 years is provide education, encouragement and guidance as an essential part of what I do.

This book, and the companion WorkBook, serve as a guide to enable you, the reader, to gain a broad outline of my perspective on why balance is integral to healing on **any and all** levels. I am hopeful you will find this to be of use to you.

I invite you to join me and begin an ongoing journey, as I share information on the art of 'Balancing Your Health' from an Holistic Integrative Medical perspective.

Balance

 Our health is an intricate balance, largely determined by the choices we make and what Love has in store for us. As I often tell my patients, I can guide you and hold your hand as you move towards 'Balancing Your Health;' ultimately, the responsibility to walk the path and take action is yours. Although focusing on Root

Cause(s) and Resolution is an important part of what we do, I know with certainty that without incorporating balance, the results might be good, but not **great**.

This is termed RCR&B©

Root Cause Resolution & Balance©.

This involves an implicit understanding that one's main issue has many facets, and though resolution is important, using a balanced approach is a great way to start.

And start we must!

Why Balance Rx©

My Signature Program—'**Balance Rx©**'—has been developed and continues to evolve during the course of my clinical career. It is the framework that forms the foundation of what I do in my practice, every day.

This program, uses 7 Keys, that each constitute an important segment of the whole, and each segment has at least seven sections. Each of these segments and sections are considered and addressed with each individual.

I have a very pragmatic side, and this is reflected in making the process and implementation of our program especially doable. Education is a big deal, and we do a lot of it!

So, before we continue, I need you to **pause,** and be ready to take action in your life. There will be several **calls to action** in this book, and this is the first. I am by nature a **pragmatist**, since I sincerely believe that dreaming about 'Balancing Your Health' is important. But equally important is the **doing**. By this I mean that taking action is fundamental to achieving those dreams!

This book asks three questions, which provide an outline and structure with specific and definite answers. I can assure you that through the thousands of patients I have had the privilege of working with, I have found that this framework **just works**.

I will outline the 3 essential questions, frame them in a particular order and provide context that I know will help you:

- Bring and define your **WHY** into being.
- Outline the framework of the **WHAT**.
- Ultimately find the **WAY** forward.

As we proceed to the first chapter, and subsequently through the book, I will show and share with you, thoughts, ideas and information on **'Balance Rx©.'**

So let's get started![1]

---

[1] I'd like to note that this small book serves as a synopsis, and is accompanied by a WorkBook which significantly expands on the material covered. Additional materials and information that are in the WorkBook will be designated with this symbol, **§**.

CHAPTER 1

A Diagnosis Should Not Be Your Destiny!

A DIAGNOSIS
SHOULD NOT
BE YOUR
DESTINY

Alexander T. Augoustides, M.D., ABIHM, FAAFP
Piedmont Integrative Medicine, PA

When you get into a tight place and everything goes against you, till it seems as though you could not hang on a minute longer, never give up then, for that is just the place and time that the tide will turn.

—Harriet Beecher Stowe

What we are talking about here is a paradigm shift. You are not defined or tied to anything, unless you **choose** to be described or diagnosed as such.

Many times in our lives pain acts as a signal that:

- We are out of balance.
- Root cause(s) needs to be resolved.
- We need healing on a particular level.

We are afraid!

Typically, our immediate reaction is to look down, but the lesson always is to learn to look up towards the source of what you believe embodies love, since:

Unconditional Love Is The Greatest Healer.

When we are in pain, at any level, we should **not** ask why!

Rather, two questions should be pondered on:

1. What does this mean?
2. What should we do?

However, when we reflect on the reframing of the **WHY** question, then this may certainly help to outline a strategy, that leads to **Root Cause Resolution, and Balance.**

We now come to the exciting part of discovering a truer understanding of the way forward: finding balance in our

Biological Footprint, which is henceforth defined as the **Triad of the Body, Mind and Spirit**.

So, what are the questions that need to be asked?

There are 3...

WHY? Now I am asking you a very simple yet complex question: What's your **WHY**? I am not referring to the futile train of logic that we all employ to decipher what is going on in our particular situation. Rather, I implore you to give heartfelt consideration to what your **imperative** is, i.e. the drive which leads you to **act** in the physical, emotional, or spiritual circumstances that you may face!

WHAT? This question refers to **WHAT** exactly is in your environment. What tools are available to you that will provide a framework for moving forward? The question you need to ask yourself is:

Are the tools that you are currently using to cope with life's challenges right for you?

HOW? We can rephrase this question as, **Where is the WAY?** How can you use the framework outlined in this book to build a lattice to success out from the situation in which you find yourself?

CHAPTER 2

Listening with The Heart & Healing With Love—My Why

We are constantly invited to be who we are.

—Henry David Thoreau

Again, I ask you WHY?

As we start our journey, we begin with the central question, the answer to which drives all the discussion and action points that follow. Why we do, feel or think something defines the route we take on the journey to 'Balance Your Health.' I will endeavor to share with you, what my **WHY** is, which will in turn give you some food for thought, as you determine your own **WHY**.

My particular **WHY** is directly determined by a number of factors that have gradually unfolded in my life.

1. I have come to see and thereby unfold my understanding of the importance of balance in all areas of our lives, specifically in the domain of my own health and that of the patients that I see.
2. I have been able to progress enthusiastically along the **road less traveled** by diligent application to a journey of studying and applying a praxis to my work that gives me great joy.

Equilibrium is always determined by a triangulated balancing of opposites. Let me explain.

The opposites in this situation are the:

1. **BIOLOGICAL FOOTPRINT** – defined as the Triad of the Body, Mind and Spirit.
2. **NATURE'S TEMPLATE** – defined as the ideal that Love's intention has for us.

The **FULCRUM** over which this process occurs rests on the particular path that one traverses in life.

Alexander T. Augoustides, M.D., ABIHM, FAAFP
Piedmont Integrative Medicine, PA

In my experience, root cause identification and progressive resolution aligned with balance are the central tenets that leads to healing.

So much so, that I have a phrase for this!

Beautiful Balance Starts At The Roots.

The image that immediately resonates with this principle is that of a **tree**. Interestingly, the etymology of this word connotes a strength of truth.

Our truth should be like all good trees, united in Body, Mind and Spirit and growing taller and wider.

Authenticity

Symbolically speaking, authenticity is the yard stick of looking for truthful answers. So, in our quest for the disturbance(s) that are **root-related**, we must adhere to the truth balanced in the barometer of the heart.

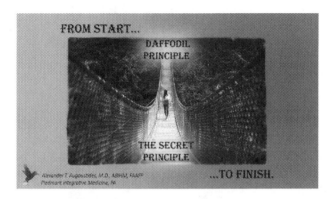

Three of the most important principles I will touch and teach on in this book are:

1. **The Daffodil Principle**
2. **The Secret Principle**
3. **The Principle of Opposites**

All of this, and much more which will be discussed further in some detail. §

We might conceptualize the quest for root cause resolution and balance as allowing the heart to show us the way. We are all here to have the opportunity to graduate in our life journey with a Ph.D. in unconditional love. As we come to understand that 'unconditional love is the greatest healer,' we are given the opportunity for root cause resolution and balance at the deepest level, in fact at all levels.

Hence, I know now why my touchstone has always been

Listening with the Heart and Healing with Love.

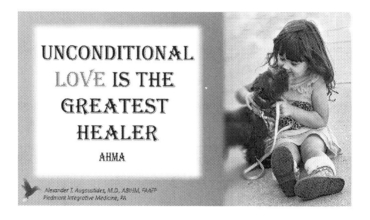

Now let's explore your **WHY** in the next chapter.

CHAPTER 3

What's Your Why?

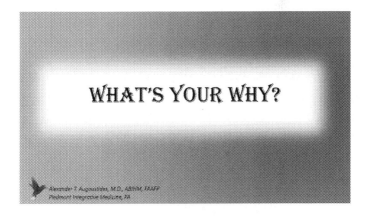

Excuses are the enemy of success, while authentic reasons are what make victory possible.

—Alexander T. Augoustides, MD, ABIHM, FAAFP

The hinge point or cornerstone of all long-lasting resolutions, decisions or action plans is your personal **WHY**. "To thine own self be true," as Polonius states in the play *Hamlet* is what I am talking about.

Authenticity is the barometer of one's personal truth, measured in the love of the heart. Truly silence is golden, as we stand in solitude and discern the whisper of the truth that is offered to us, in this sacred space.

This yardstick can also help us interpret our daily emotional ups and downs as undulant 'weather,' which is always at the level of our false self, our **personality**. However, our **authenticity**, also known as our **truth**, is a reflection of our real 'climate' i.e. what we stand for, and what is important to us.

We all need to understand that the root cause of a disturbance in our inner peace is **fear**.

Fear-based thinking is always conditioned and confined by an anticipation of consequence whether good or bad. Actions that are conditioned by consequence, are by their nature, limiting. So, when we say we are happy

or sad, these statements are conditional, precisely on the perceived happenings in our environment. The heart is the place where we can access a type of mindset that is unconditional. Thus, this journey grants us access to a state of freedom; that is true joy—which allows us to resonate with our *raison d'etre*—our **WHY**.

We could write volumes of prose and poetry on how this needs to occur, and more importantly **WHY**! But for brevity's sake, I would like to share with you the Serenity Prayer, an intrinsic beacon in my own spiritual journey, which has helped answer the question of balance in my own thoughts.

So why define and decide on your unique **WHY?**

1. Your **WHY** gives you an authentic starting point.
2. When you flounder, and you will, you have an anchor that you can reach back to, which gives you the  wherewithal to stay the course you have decided and chosen.

In my experience, I have found that the majority of my patients need a plan that is **practical** and most importantly, **doable**. The fact that you have decided to read this material indicates on many levels a yearning for wholeness and healing on your part. So let's continue with this as your focus.

Now we come to the most important question in this book- understanding and knowing your **WHY** with absolute certainty. You need clarity, confidence and courage!

One of the most fundamental tools that are used to build the bridge to one's **WHY** is a **JOURNAL.** §[2] This provides the space and necessary infrastructure to:

- ○ Continually return and 'work on' your vision(the Daffodil Principle).
- ○ Create accountability, the cornerstone of continuous successful implementation.

---

[2] I have expanded upon this concept by providing a list of journals in the Work Book.

○ Add in strategies that you find work for you.
○ Take out strategies that may serve as barriers to personal growth.
○ Explore and learn how to grow.
○ Serve as a template for the design and nurturing of the seedling of your **WHY** into the tree of the version of a balanced you.
○ Bring together the forces of your intellect (logical) and intuition (understanding).

I have outlined my thoughts on my WHY, now I ask you to do the same.

To this end, you need to now, pause and take action. By this I mean, putting on the table **actionable items** which you know need to be done to make this vision take root in the reality that you find yourself.

I have outlined the 3 essential questions, and have framed them in a particular order and context which I know will help you define your WHY. §[3]

---

[3] These questions are greatly elaborated on with the worksheets in the workbook.

Why Are You Here?

What Are Your Dreams For Your Life Canvas?

_____

_____

_____

_____

_____

Where Does Your Health Fit In This Canvas?

_____

_____

_____

_____

_____

CHAPTER 4

The What—The 7 Keys Framework

KEY (kē)

(n.) - an instrument for opening locks

Etymology of Key

From the Middle English —"keie," descending from the Old English "cæg," a metal piece that works a lock[4]

We come now to the bridge between your **WHY** and the **WAY**. So, like all explorers we ask more questions and pick those that resonate with our **WHY** and can be implemented in a way that is congruent with our heart's resonance. This will involve a discussion of tips and tools that will unpack your ability to discern the detail of **what is available to you to provide a framework** with which you can begin your journey.

There is a plethora of information available to each of us, and there is no benefit in being overwhelmed. What is needed is a Key, instead of a sledgehammer to open the door to any new endeavor or exploration of the options at hand. When swamped with a flood of information, we have a choice.

We can approach it with either a:

- State of **panic.**
Or
- Calm understanding.

---

[4] "Key (N.1)." *Etymonline*, Douglas Harper, www.etymonline.com/word/key.

I like to think of the panic as a 'sympathetic overdrive,' the revving up of the engine of our logical mindset. That peace or calm understanding can best be defined as a state of coherence (an inner knowing that we are grateful to be able to participate, and to have given our best which emerges from the Relaxation Response, the parasympathetic calm. [5]

This balanced approach, is congruent with the term **elegance**. Thus we use a Key, and not a sledgehammer!

---

[5] **Autonomic Nervous System (ANS)**. The ANS regulates a variety of involuntary (take place with no conscious effort), body functions - such as heartbeat, blood flow, breathing, and digestion.

There are 3 branches of the ANS:

1. The sympathetic system
2. The parasympathetic system
3. The enteric nervous system

The sympathetic division regulates the flight-or-fight responses. This division also performs such tasks as relaxing the bladder, speeding up heart rate and dilating the pupils of the eye. The parasympathetic division helps maintain normal body functions and conserves physical resources (Relaxation) such as controlling the bladder, slowing down heart rate and constricting the pupils of the eye. The third section, the enteric nervous system, is confined to the gastrointestinal tract. Our resilience is important, particularly when confronted with a potentially threatening situation. The ability to maintain a state of Autonomic Nervous System (ANS) Balance is an important marker for one's state of Mind and Body balance.

This ideal state of resilience is called **coherence.** "'Coherence is the state when the heart, mind and emotions are in energetic alignment and cooperation,' HeartMath Institute Research Director Dr. Rollin McCraty says."[6]

This discussion is particularly important as you approach your **WHAT**, and in fact all three questions of your **WHY**, **WHAT** and **WHERE IS THE WAY**. There needs to be a state of **coherence** within your Biological Footprint.

---

[6] "Coherence." *HeartMath Institute*, HeartMath Institute, 2 Mar. 2015, www.heartmath.org/articles-of-the-heart/the-math-of-heartmath/coherence/.

$$C = R \& C$$

Alexander T. Augoustides, M.D., ABIHM, FAAFP
Piedmont Integrative Medicine, PA

This equation describes the components of coherence:

Coherence = Congruence & Resonance

- **Coherence** = balanced resilience
- **Resonance** = intuitive, emotional - knowing (heart)
- **Congruence** = logical, intellectual knowing head

So, when you are coming to a decision there needs to be balanced coherence which is a harmony of knowing that takes the intellect and the intuition into account. That's how you just know.

Again, a more detailed discussion is outside the scope of this small book, but is dealt with in-depth in the accompanying WorkBook.

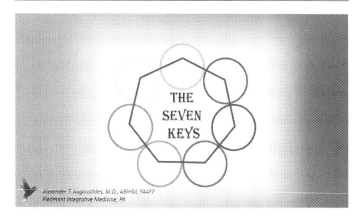

This optimized balance is conceptualized best by:

'Balance Rx©'

As we continue with this guide to 'Balancing Your Health,' we now arrive in more detail to the Secret Principle. So, what is the Secret Principle? Over the last 20 years, I have distilled the quintessence of what works in my Holistic Integrative Medical practice with a scalable, malleable system that I use multiple times every day.

The Secret Principle is the backbone of the '**7 Keys**,' the foundation of the signature program I have now named the '**Balance Rx©,**' which forms the framework for my patients and essentially anyone who is looking to balance their health. The '**7 Keys**' form a composite solution to equilibrium in the domain of one's health. Each key is unique in its own contribution; together they form a balanced whole.

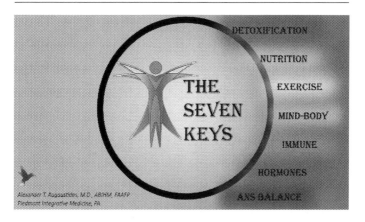

As you have come to see so far, the focus of this book and my own application of Holistic Integrative Medicine is **balance** and **coherence**. The logical lattice or **congruence** that 'Balance Rx©' follows is the '**7 Keys**' which I have defined as **Detoxification, Nutrition, Exercise, Mind-Body, Immune, Hormones,** and **ANS Balance.** The **resonance** or intuitive bent to my style of practice is that I think of my signature program in sections (each key) and segments (the components of the respective key). Each unique Biological Footprint that I interact with is made up of a varying combination of key sections and respective segments.

In the next chapter, I want to focus on this Mind-Body Key segment: the journey from Fear to Love. This will allow you to see the importance of balance and coherence in how you ask and begin to answer the three questions.

CHAPTER 5

From Fear To Love— The Mind/Body Key

If you knew the secret of life, you too would choose no other companion but love.

—Rumi

In the journey through life, and in situations where we may be faced with decisions and difficulties, making choices from the perspective of love is always the best. We are told that hate is the opposite of love; ultimately, we hate what we **fear**. In the same way we often have to hit ourselves on the head, so that our heart has a chance to be heard! **Stress** is the antithesis of **Serenity**, and balancing these two opposites is what I have termed **Stress Shifting**©. [7]

Sacred Secret Garden

> *"The enemy is fear. We think it is hate; but, it is fear."*

—*Mahatma Gandhi*

STRESS SHIFTING

THE CONTENT & CONNECTED GARDNER

Alexander T. Augoustides, M.D., ABIHM, FAAFP
Piedmont Integrative Medicine, PA

---

[7] This is a key concept in the Mind/Body section of the 7 Keys – and in particular the Fear/Love segment. §

Fear based activity is often frenetic and frantic, and is termed: 'the chaotic madness of doing!'

Over the years, as I have pondered about **Stress Shifting©**, the concept of a **Sacred Secret Garden** has grown in my heart. As we journey through our lives, we need constant renewal and refreshment. By nurturing and developing the garden of our body, mind, and spirit, we can revitalize and recreate our weary selves.

When stressed on a higher level, our inner sanctuary is where we travel to, and if done daily this does serve as a source of restoration.

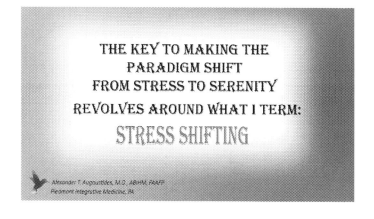

Starting with an *Attitude of Gratitude* and getting rid of the *Stinkin' Thinkin'* further enables the cultivation of mental and emotional peace.

We need to move toward becoming transparent to the love we all have in us and allow ourselves and others those moments of caring and kindness. Participating in prayer and meditation on a daily basis, reading spiritual material that is relevant to our personal beliefs and serving others are the bedrock of this journey. We should endeavor to create that special quiet time in the **Sacred Secret Garden** of the heart where we can revitalize, rejuvenate and recreate our biological constitution on all levels.

Start Living

Realize the dream within you.

—Alexander T. Augoustides, MD, ABIHM, FAAFP

Fear based thinking constricts your heart, and pushes your Biological Footprint into an ANS (Autonomic Nervous System) state of Sympathetic Dominance. Love on the other hand opens the door of the heart and facilitates a 'Relaxation Response' in the parasympathetic component of the ANS, which then allows for the emergence of coherence. As you are asking the three questions, this process will inevitably lead you to an examination of your state of healthful balance.

The 'Art of Balance' serves as the platform for living. We know that we should *stop dreaming and start living*. However, just the opposite may also be in order: *start dreaming, and start living*.

The Three Brains

For there is nothing either Good or Bad, but thinking makes it so.

—Shakespeare

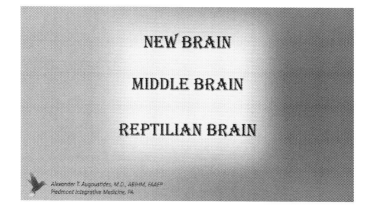

NEW BRAIN

MIDDLE BRAIN

REPTILIAN BRAIN

Alexander T. Augoustides, M.D., ABIHM, FAAFP
Piedmont Integrative Medicine, PA

An important part of understanding how we direct our thoughts and how they are connected to our emotions, and subsequent actions, is model of the **triune brain**.[8]

[8] Kazlev, M.Alan. "The Triune Brain." *Paul MacLean's Triune Brain Hypothesis*, M.Alan Kazlev, 19 Mar. 1999, www.kheper. net/topics/intelligence/MacLean.htm.

Reptilian Brain (including basal ganglia, mid-brain, and brainstem): principally associated with physical survival and maintenance. It controls questions like fight or flight. In addition to real threats, perceived threats are as important, and this becomes integral since a defining factor of our overall balance is the constant mental chatter that is fear-based that churns in our heads.

Middle Brain (including the amygdala, hippocampus, hypothalamus and other structures in the *limbic system*): primarily senses the reality you are engaged in through emotions and feelings.

New Brain (neocortex): logically analyzes all information presented to it. This is also known as the thinking brain.

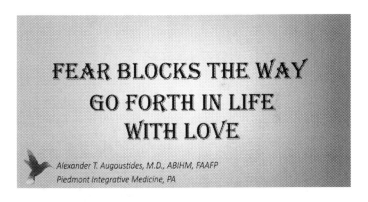

FEAR BLOCKS THE WAY
GO FORTH IN LIFE
WITH LOVE

Alexander T. Augoustides, M.D., ABIHM, FAAFP
Piedmont Integrative Medicine, PA

The main reason I have outlined the 'three brain' model is to focus on two areas that are critically tied in with the whole discussion about the journey from fear to love—the **ANS** (Autonomic Nervous System) and the **Amygdala**.

The Amygdala

The amygdala (*Greek word – Almond*), is situated in the temporal lobe of the brain and is part of the limbic system, a neural network in the middle brain with many complex connections. The amygdala may be thought of as the collective center that integrates emotions, motivation and emotional behavior. It has an essential role in decoding threatening stimuli.

Aggravation of this area, whether perceived or real, causes intense emotion such as fear or aggression.

Of interest to this discussion is the function of the amygdala that is related to control of the Autonomic Nervous System responses associated with fear.

Deer in the Headlights

The amygdala processes sensory input, and generates a response to fear through connections with the ANS. So this typical fight, flight or freeze response is  modulated between the interaction of complex neural circuitry involving the amygdala and the ANS.

Matter Over Heart

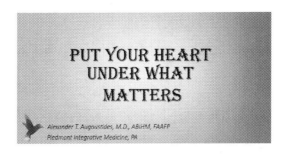

Mind over Matter, while important, can be a logical discursive rumination and is usually the most common mode of thinking that quite frankly can leave one exhausted. Consider peeking outside the box and taking the perspective of putting your heart under what matters. This will allow your logical mind to enter the intuitive domain of the heart and allow more **coherence** into the framework of your question.

The Filter of Love

The journey that we undertake daily is part of what we all do. Unfoldment of your heart's intent is what the game of life is all about. However, the field of the mind is where most of us spend a significant amount of time, during our daily grind. Speaking of grinds, an analogy may be useful. We can actively choose what to filter our day with in every moment. So, in the same way when we make a cup of delicious coffee, a filter is used to keep the coffee grounds out of our cup of Java. As you go through your day, consider filtering out the 'grounds' of your negativity and fears with the active choice to embody love in what you think, feel and do.

Gardening

The whole process of balancing one's Biological Footprint centers around the interaction between one's Biological Footprint and Nature's Template. The importance of this cannot be over emphasized.

A useful metaphorical snapshot is the following regarding the three rules of Gardening:

1. Lay out and nurture the best garden you can.
2. Look at the weeds, identify the big ones and take care of them.

3. Once you have laid out your garden and taken care of the big weeds, get on your knees and pray for rain.

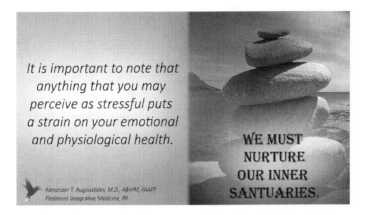

It is important to note that anything that you may perceive as stressful puts a strain on your emotional and physiological health.

Alexander T. Augoustides, M.D., ABIHM, FAAFP
Piedmont Integrative Medicine, PA

WE MUST
NURTURE
OUR INNER
SANTUARIES.

So maybe one way of looking at this would be to frame this in the context of the discussion of this book:

- **Laying out** your best garden is taken to mean asking and answering your three questions, and acting on that information with a structured, sustainable plan of action.
- The **weeds** are those instances where more homework is needed. I stress that one cannot and should not address all the problematic areas. Rather, one should rely on the concept of leverage. This principle says that the 'action' of solving the significant 20% of one's problematic areas actually impacts the state of 'being' of the remaining 80%.
- The **rain** of Love's intention for us is central to the success of all gardening. It is called God's Grace

by many and in general, refers to our efforts to produce growth in alignment with Love's intended direction for our continuing optimal blossoming.

Our best effort coupled with Love's intention is an important principle here.

1. Good garden and no rain = no growth
2. Good rain and no garden = no growth

So it's only a synergistic interaction between our work with our **Biological Footprint** (work in the garden) and **Nature's Template** (Love's intention and direction), that allows for **RCR&B©** to occur on all levels.

The Healing Perspective of Gratitude

So where is your focus? The way you determine your focus is critical to a balanced perspective of the whole.

Given the constant stress that we respond to, the Adrenal Glands can become fatigued which indicates suboptimal function.

The emotion of Gratitude grounds the Adrenals. We come to view the proverbial cup as half-full, instead of half-empty. This change of view on all levels moves us profoundly from the mental state of scarcity to plenty with the corresponding signaling of Fear to Love, being predominant. This is ultimately what I have come to understand by **Stress Shifting©**. The balanced approach to move from either mode of the ANS—Sympathetic (Active/Red Zone) or Parasympathetic (Passive/Green

Zone) to a state of coherence(Resilience/Orange Zone). Another visualization would be that of a traffic light 🚦.

So why is such emphasis being placed on the journey from fear to love. Quite simply because the root resolution of our pain lies in this journey and the balance in our biological milieu that is attainable by each and every one of us.

Driving Forward

As we move onto the next chapter, we start to close the journey of the three questions that we have started in this book. Before we do that though, I want to bring another quality of the river which runs through your life to your attention. My hope for you as you consider these questions and their answers is that you rekindle what drives you forward, your **enthusiasm** (joyful connection with Love's Intention). Consider the quote from Huie that a river cuts through rock, not because of its power, but because of its persistence. As we come to the next chapter, you will find a story that is pregnant with meaning, and full of possibility as you take the next step toward understanding my perspective on balancing your health.

CHAPTER 6

The Daffodil Principle— Persistence Girded With Patience

Through a long and painful process, I've learned that happiness is an inside job— not based on anything or anyone in the outer material world.

I've become a different and better person— not perfect, but still a work in progress.

—Alana Stewart

The Tortoise always wins the race.

Among, many patients I have had the privilege of connecting with, the answer to one question that I ask is always the same: in the fable of the tortoise and hare, who wins the race? To this point, and the thousands of times that I have asked this question, the tortoise **ALWAYS** wins the race! Slowly, but surely, with a road map in hand the tortoise crosses the finish line. How many times have we heard about goals and getting there? This question and its answer are another example of how everyone wants an instant fix, **NOW**.

Ponder on This...

If you are given a house, versus making the payment on the house each month for 30 years, I ask you - 'Who owns this house?' In the first instance, you had to do nothing; you just got the house. In the second instance, you did something significant; you did the work to make each of those payments. Therefore, in the second instance, there is responsibility, accountability and consistency in the doing of whatever was necessary to make the payment. We need to bring that process to bear on your desire to balance your health, an activity that you know is worthwhile. Afterall, that is why you are reading this book!

This now allows us to explore the **DAFFODIL PRINCIPLE,** which ultimately is a call to small, sustainable incremental goal-oriented actions. Remember action without enthusiasm, or an understanding that there is a framework is futile since it is not goal-directed.

A Summary of this Principle

The Daffodil Principle is a short story where a daughter takes her reluctant, busy mother on a trip to a nearby field. The mother gazes in wonder at five acres of daffodils (50,000) that have been planted, one day at a time, by one woman, over 40 years.

Here is a short excerpt from the mother's perspective:

> *For me, that moment was a life-changing experience. I thought of this woman whom I had never met, who almost fifty years before, had begun, one bulb at a time, to bring her vision of beauty and joy to an obscure mountaintop. Planting one bulb*

at a time, year after year, this unknown woman had forever changed the world in which she lived. One day at a time, she had created something of extraordinary magnificence, beauty and inspiration.

The principle her daffodil garden taught is one of the greatest principles of celebration—that is, learning to move toward our goals and desires one step at a time, often just one baby step at a time and learning to love the doing, learning to use the accumulation of time.

"It makes me sad in a way," I admitted to Carolyn (her daughter). "What might I have accomplished if I had thought of a wonderful goal thirty-five years or forty years ago and had worked away at it one bulb at a time through all those years? Just think what I might have been able to achieve!"

My daughter summed up the message of the day in her usual direct way. "Start tomorrow," she said. She was right. It's so pointless to think of the lost hours of yesterdays.

How can I put this to use today?

WILL YOU WAIT....

UNTIL YOUR CAR OR HOME IS PAID OFF
UNTIL YOU GET A NEW CAR OR HOME
UNTIL YOUR KIDS LEAVE THE HOUSE
UNTIL YOU FINISH SCHOOL
UNTIL YOU CLEAN THE HOUSE
UNTIL YOU ORGANIZE THE GARAGE
UNTIL YOU CLEAN OFF YOUR DESK
UNTIL YOU LOSE 10 LBS.
UNTIL YOU GAIN 10 LBS.
UNTIL YOU GET MARRIED
UNTIL YOU GET A DIVORCE
UNTIL YOU HAVE KIDS
UNTIL THE KIDS GO TO SCHOOL
UNTIL YOU RETIRE
UNTIL SUMMER
UNTIL SPRING
UNTIL WINTER
UNTIL FALL

UNTIL YOU DIE

Alexander T. Augoustides, MD FAAFP ABIHM
Piedmont Integrative Medicine, PA

CHAPTER 7

The Way—The 7 Keys Unpacked

Setting Goals is the first step in turning the Invisible into the Visible.

—*Tony Robbins*

We now arrive at the last chapter, and the answer to the third question: **Where is the Way**. This question can only be answered, once the other two are pondered on and taken in sequence. This may sound obvious, but one can only climb a ladder step by step. The encouraging thing is that there is a way, that's doable and produces results. Going through a door can be done in one of two ways:

1. With a Sledgehammer
2. A Key

Clearly, both methods work! However almost to a fault, my patients prefer the Key. This reminds me of a scene in the movie *Good Will Hunting* where Will looks at the complex calculus on the blackboard. After all the students have applied their sledgehammers in intellectual futility, he is able to see the Key and writes down the solution in one line! That's what I am talking about!

So, there are many ways to kill the proverbial cat. The way forward must resonate with your heart and be congruent to your intellect. However, you have to take the first step. That's the act of trust, that allows as Tony Robbins so eloquently states, the invisible to become visible.

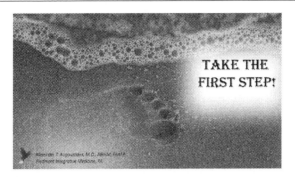

Take the FIRST STEP

If one advances confidently in the direction of his dreams and endeavors to live the life which he has imagined, he will meet with a success unexpected in common hours.

—Henry David Thoreau

So, we need to move confidently in a direction determined by your vision! Work at this with earnest endeavor and bring into the visible, from the invisible, that which has been imagined. The most beautiful part of this journey is that your efforts will be met with unexpected success. A most eloquent summation of:

Do your best, and God will take care of the rest.

Where is the Way

The first step towards getting somewhere is to decide that you are not going to stay where you are.

—Chauncey Depew

We now arrive at the explication of one way that over almost 20 years of clinical practice and experience, I have found eminently useful. As you have seen, I lay great emphasis on the balance of the analysis and implementation of the findings into a canvas that allows progress towards healing on all levels of one's Biological Footprint. I will now outline the process we use in our clinic which I am hopeful will be helpful for you as a paradigm to serve as a guide on your journey as you make a packing list for your itinerary. So get ready to pack your suitcase!

BALANCE RX©

A Holistic Integrative Medical Paradigm

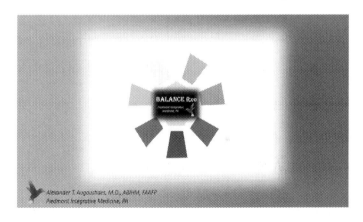

What is the difference between a **Program** and **Paradigm**? To further help in your understanding, a program is something that is written and put forth, and a paradigm is a model of example. So, what we need to consider in context is the example of the **'Balance Rx©'** that is now being written out, and how this may serve you as an illustration of what is to be expected.

When I sit down with a patient, I am pondering on three key metrics:

1. What the patient I am with is telling me regarding their situation and/or problems
2. What I see and discern, in the context of their story
3. Any lab work, imaging or other testing

This forms the entry point to the ongoing encounter and the formulation of a program of balance that is unique to that particular person.

While many solutions aim for Root Cause Resolution (RCR), I firmly believe that the balance between one's Biological Footprint and Nature's Template is implicit not only for RCR, but for **ONGOING** Resolution of the problem(s). So I have included this concept in what we try to achieve which is

Root Cause Resolution & Balance (RCR&B©).

In fact, I now do not talk about the concept of guiding an individual to resolution of whatever issues they are dealing with. Rather, we talk about and move towards a unique point of balance for that individual that may/not include full RCR. This perspective allows for a realistic outcome and expectations on behalf of the patient and the provider.

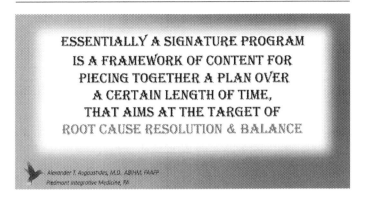

ESSENTIALLY A SIGNATURE PROGRAM
IS A FRAMEWORK OF CONTENT FOR
PIECING TOGETHER A PLAN OVER
A CERTAIN LENGTH OF TIME,
THAT AIMS AT THE TARGET OF
ROOT CAUSE RESOLUTION & BALANCE

Alexander T. Augoushides, M.D., ABIHM, FAAFP
Piedmont Integrative Medicine, PA

I am able to outline and formulate a program for a particular individual. Although, oftentimes the variables of that individual's effort, and Love's intention for that individual can only unfold and be determined with time.

The process of formulation of each unique program goes through four steps that I will share with you.

THE SEVEN KEYS

DETOXIFICATION
NUTRITION
EXERCISE
MIND-BODY
IMMUNE
HORMONES
ANS BALANCE

CLINICAL TESTING
EDUCATION SERVICES

Alexander T. Augoushides, M.D., ABIHM, FAAFP
Piedmont Integrative Medicine, PA

PART 1

We start with a **ROF** (Review of Findings). This consists of an evaluation and assessment done in the context of an office visit where:

- We review the completed Intake Questionnaire.
- I meaningfully discuss the prospective patient's case with them.
- A comprehensive examination of the patient is done.

Next we do an analysis of all data including lab work, imaging and any other information that is pertinent to the case.

What follows then is a discussion and presentation of what I determine to be the patient's main issues and problems.

Finally, we discuss and act on a comprehensive solution with various options unique to each individual. This then serves as a fulcrum to make a start.

PART 2

PART 2
WE LAY A LATTICE

BALANCE. Rx©
A Holistic Integrative Program Paradigm

DETOXIFICATION
NUTRITION
EXERCISE
MIND-BODY
IMMUNE
HORMONES
ANS-BALANCE

Alexander T. Augoustides, M.D., ABIHM, FAAFP
Piedmont Integrative Medicine, PA.

Here, over time, and at the initial consultation the following are reviewed:

- The various sections of each of the **'7 Keys'**
- The segments of each Key

This forms the framework for:

1. Discussion of which sections and segment(s) are the most pertinent to this individual.
2. Ongoing education with respect to where, as a team, we need to focus to achieve the goal of **RCR&B©** (Root Cause Resolution & Balance).

PART 3

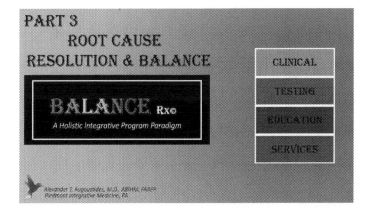

PART 3
ROOT CAUSE
RESOLUTION & BALANCE

BALANCE Rx©
A Holistic Integrative Program Paradigm

CLINICAL

TESTING

EDUCATION

SERVICES

Alexander T. Augoustides, M.D., ABIHM, FAAFP
Piedmont Integrative Medicine, PA

This part serves as a **launchpad** for **RCR&B©** (Root Cause Resolution & Balance). During the next three to twelve months, and depending on the number and the severity of the **RCP**(Root Cause Problem[s]), the following occurs:

Clinical

Clinical consists of serial office visits, where over the course of time, the various problems are addressed and balanced by my staff, and I.

Testing

Depending on what the issues are, testing is done to gain a comprehensive understanding of the:

- Hormonal
- Immune/Gut
- Detoxification
- Sections/Segments that are identified as being important for the individual

Education

The patient is given resources, and consultation about:

- Nutrition
- Exercise
- Mind Body Continuum
- Hormones
- Detoxification

Services

These depend on the review of findings, and the longitudinal determination and analysis of test results and clinical findings. Think of this as 'menu' items that are chosen and accessed during the treatment term by our clinical team.

These may include ongoing testing, supplements/nutraceuticals, and any other service/product/program that is going to contribute to **RCR&B©** (Root Cause Resolution & Balance).

PART 4

PART 4

BALANCE Rx©
A Holistic Integrative Program Paradigm

THE SEVEN

KEYS

Alexander T. Augoustides, MD FAAFP ABIHM
Piedmont Integrative Medicine, PA

Here, we focus on two areas, on ongoing **RCR&B©** (Root Cause Resolution & Balance), and maintenance of what we have worked so hard at trying to achieve. An optimized unique balance point between one's Biological Footprint and Nature's Template is the narrow way that Piedmont Integrative Medicine, PA and I are determined to help our patients find. From here, we strive to help you thrive with a lattice built for longitudinal success.

CONCLUSION & THE NEXT STEP

So What's Next?

"Life is like riding a bicycle. To keep your balance, you must keep moving."

—*Albert Einstein*

It's time to start living the life you've imagined.

—*Henry James*

I close this book with gratitude.

Firstly, that I have had a chance to write this, and secondly to share with you what works. As we outlined in this book (and in significantly more detail in the WorkBook):

1. The Three Key Questions
2. The Daffodil Principle
3. The Secret Principle—The 7 Keys
4. A Coherent Lattice For Success

No one item is more important than the other but together they form a template that will, if applied, give you the reader the opportunity to 'Balance Your Health.'

Our lives are defined by search and ultimate use of the good, the beautiful and the true. As Black Elk of the Oglala Lakota says, "May you always walk in Beauty."

I would readily add,

"May you walk in Beauty, allowing the Truth
to shine forth in your Goodness."

*Take That Next Step
which will allow you to
step out in confidence,
Balance Your Health,
and Sing Your Song!*

ABOUT THE AUTHOR

Alexander T. Augoustides, MD, ABIHM, FAAFP

Alexander Augoustides, MD or simply 'Dr. A' has been in private practice since 1993 and has a solid background in Family Medicine with a special interest in Holistic Integrative Medicine. Dr. A earned his medical degree from the University of Cape Town, South Africa, and completed his residency at Marshall University School of Medicine in Huntington, West Virginia, where he served as Chief Resident. Following this, he completed a family practice teaching fellowship program at ETSU in Johnson City, Tennessee.

A practicing physician, Dr. Augoustides has continued the legacy of his clinic, Piedmont Integrative Medicine, PA, which was established in 1984 under the leadership of Dr. Walter A. Ward. 'Dr. A' took over stewardship of the clinic in 2004. Over the last 20 years, he has journeyed both personally and professionally in balancing the health of his patients. This has been the foundation for the **'Balance Rx©'** program at Piedmont Integrative Medicine, PA.

Outside of his clinical practice, 'Dr. A' enjoys photography in Reynolda Gardens, swimming and ocean kayaking, soaking up the sun on any NC beach, and attending church with his family. When asked what his life mantra is, he usually replies,

"I simply go with the flow."

Printed in the United States
By Bookmasters